The
Fisherman

ISBN 979-8-89345-167-2 (paperback)
ISBN 979-8-89345-168-9 (digital)

Christian Faith Publishing
832 Park Avenue
Meadville, PA 16335
www.christianfaithpublishing.com

Printed in the United States of America

The Fisherman

Michelle Elizabeth

There once lived a man named Simon. He and his brother Andrew were great fishermen. Day after day, they sailed the Sea of Galilee, dropping their nets and catching the most magnificent fish.

2

One dark and misty night, Simon and Andrew traveled out into the deep sea to do some fishing. They stayed up all night, dropping their heavy nets into the sea, desperately hoping they would catch some fish. They tried, and strived, and struggled. Their arms ached. Their hands were covered with blisters from dropping and lifting their massive nets over and over and over.

Night turned into morning, and to their disappointment, they had not caught any fish.

As they returned to dry land to wash their nets, they noticed a mysterious man standing on the shore surrounded by a huge crowd of people. The crowd was so big that they were pushing the man into the sea. *Who was this man?* they thought. *And why were so many people crowded around him?*

Simon and his brother docked their boat along the shore beside the crowd that huddled around the mysterious man. As Simon washed his nets, he looked up and saw the man standing next to him.

He smiled and politely asked, "May I board your boat?"

Simon had a good heart, so he agreed to let him on the boat to protect him from the crowd.

Upon boarding the boat, the man looked at Simon. "Row out a little distance from the shore," he directed in a calm but compelling voice.

There was something special about this man, and for some strange reason, Simon trusted him. So he rowed out from the shore as the man had requested.

The man sat down on the boat and started teaching the crowd. Simon listened to the man teach as he continued to wash his nets. His words were kind but powerful. Simon had never heard a teacher speak like this before.

With his last word to the crowd, the man turned to Simon and said, "Row out further, into the deep water, and drop your fishing nets for a catch," as he got off the boat and returned to the shore.

Simon had little faith that there were any fish in the entire sea, for he and his brother had been trying all night to catch some, and each time they brought up their nets, they were empty. Simon lowered his head. "We've worked hard all night and caught nothing. But because you say so, I'll drop the nets," he grumbled. Simon just knew there would be no fish swimming into his nets, and he would be left feeling like a failure once again.

Simon rowed into the deep water and dropped his nets. *Nothing will be different this time*, he told himself as he plopped down in the boat. He felt defeated already.

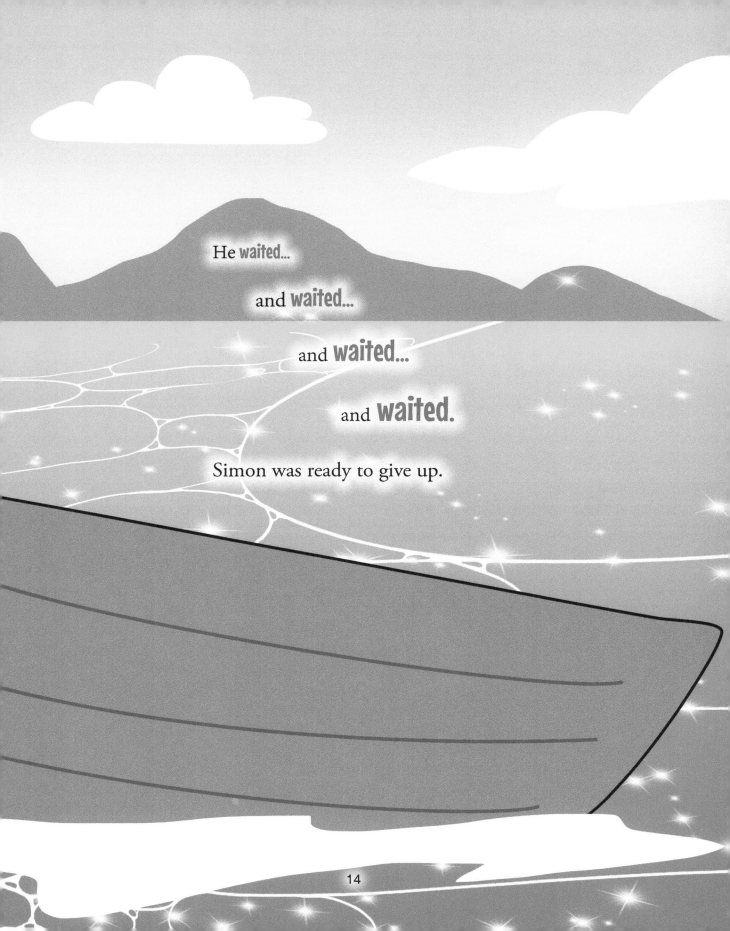

He waited...

and waited...

and waited...

and waited.

Simon was ready to give up.

Suddenly, he felt tugging on his nets, and the boat started to sway. The boat rocked more and more, tipping further and further to one side. Before Simon could rise to his feet, his nets were stuffed full with countless fish. So many fish that the nets began to break! Andrew and another group of fishermen nearby saw what was happening and raced to the boat as fast as they could to help Simon bring in his big heap of fish. They tugged the nets with all their might, and before their very eyes, the boat was filled with fish! Everyone was amazed! How could this happen? The man who was once teaching the crowd quietly watched from the shore.

Simon rowed back to the shore, got out of his boat, and staggered to the man in disbelief. The man's name was Jesus. Simon dropped to his knees and cried, "I am a bad man! I did not believe you, and you should leave me!" Simon was sorry he couldn't trust Jesus.

Jesus gently said to Simon, "Do not be afraid. From now on, you will be a fisher of men. Follow me!"

Fisher of men: someone who tells people about Jesus.

18

The moment they heard those words, Simon, Andrew, and the other fishermen left everything behind and followed Jesus wherever he went, for they knew that only he could make the impossible possible.

What do fish take to stay healthy?

Vitamin sea.

Read it! God tells us many times in the Bible how he can make the impossible possible. In Matthew 19:26, it says, "Jesus looked at them and said, 'With man this is impossible, but with God all things are possible.'"

Think it! Has there ever been a time when you were asked to do something you thought was impossible? Sometimes it can be easy to give up on things when we think they are too hard. But there is good news! We have someone special on our side, and his name is Jesus. Next time you think something is impossible, repeat this truth to yourself: "With God, all things are possible." Say it as many times as you need. Remember how Jesus works miracles, and trust that he will help you do hard things. Don't give up!

Pray it! Dear heavenly father, you are so amazing! You make all things possible, even when things seem too hard for me. Remind me every day that I can count on you to help me with the things I think I cannot do. Help me to be strong enough to tell others about the miracles you can bring. I love you with all my heart. In Jesus's name, I pray, amen.

Therefore I tell you, whatever you ask for in prayer, believe that you have received it, and it will be yours.

—Mark 11:24

About the Author

Michelle Elizabeth is an elementary school teacher with a specialty in English as a second language education. When she is not teaching, she enjoys reading, writing, serving at her local church, and spending time with her family. She and her son currently live in Texas, where she hopes to write more books like *The Fisherman* and spread God's word to children all over the world.

Printed in the USA
CPSIA information can be obtained
at www.ICGtesting.com
LVHW071729300824
789716LV00011B/42

9 798893 451672